# I Wrote This Book about You!

## Created By:

_____

_____

## Year: _____

# The Life Graduate Publishing Group

We love to receive reviews from our customers. If you had the opportunity to provide a review we would greatly appreciate it. Thank you!

**Copyright 2020 - The Life Graduate Publishing Group**

No part of this book may be scanned, reproduced or distributed in any printed or electronic form without the prior permission of the author or publisher.

# ABOUT THE AUTHOR

**My Name :**

**My Age :**

**I wrote this book about you because :**

# I LOVE YOU BECAUSE...

# THIS IS A TRACE OF MY HAND

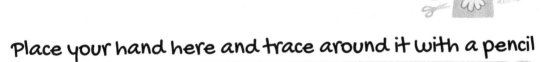

Place your hand here and trace around it with a pencil

# MY FAVORITE PLACE TO VISIT WITH YOU IS....

_____

_____

_____

_____

_____

# You like to relax by doing this.. *RELAX*

_____

_____

_____

_____

_____

# THIS IS MY FAVORITE PHOTO OF US

Stick your favorite photo here!

# THIS IS A DRAWING OF US TOGETHER

# These are 3 things you do that are kind.

1. _____

2. _____

3. _____

# We celebrate your birthday on..

MONTH _____

DAY _____

I love birthday cake!!

# You cook the best......

# My favorite story you have told me was...

I love stories!!

# I'm very brave but... I still get a little scared when...

# I would like you to show me how to...

# Your favorite time of the year is...

[                              ]

# because....

[                              ]

# This is a drawing of us together at..

# I think you are the best at....

# Your favorite food is....

# If I could get you anything in the whole wide world it would be...

# I hope that one day we can......

# I think you look like

<br>

# from the T.V !

# If I designed a T-Shirt for you, it would say this...

# My Special Design!

# You taught me how to....

# You can do this better than anyone else!

# SPECIAL MOMENTS

Add other special photo's or drawings here

# SPECIAL MOMENTS

Add other special photo's or drawings here

# THIS HAS BEEN MY SPECIAL GIFT THAT I HAVE CREATED FROM ME TO YOU. I HOPE YOU LIKE IT!

My autograph

# A Selection Of Other Books In The Series

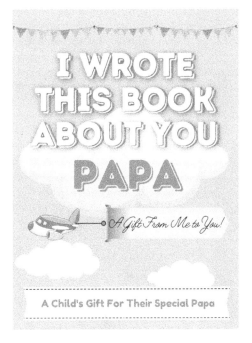

www.thelifegraduate.com

Printed in the USA
CPSIA information can be obtained
at www.ICGtesting.com
LVHW072149281123
765234LV00012B/289